Investigate Math

Grade 4

by Cindi Mitchell

Editor: Maria L. Chang
Cover design: Cynthia Ng
Interior design: Grafica, Inc.
Cover images © Shutterstock.com.
Interior art: Mike Moran (4, 21); Noun Project (41)

ISBN: 978-1-338-75171-0
Scholastic Inc., 557 Broadway, New York, NY 10012

Table of Contents

Introduction

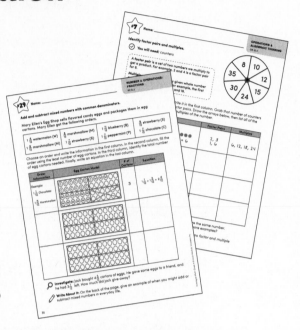

Welcome to *Investigate Math*! This book offers dozens of engaging activities designed to give students multiple opportunities to deeply investigate math concepts. Instead of memorizing algorithms and facts to solve a math problem, students need to look at the problem from various angles and see how new concepts fit into what they already know about mathematics. They need to apply their learning in different ways, brainstorm how to solve problems, shift to a new strategy when the current one is not working, and understand abstract concepts. In other words, they need to develop flexible thinking skills.

In its 2012 global survey, the Programme for International Student Assessment (PISA) found that in every country students who memorized mathematical concepts were the lowest achievers. Students who use relational strategies and self-monitoring may initially struggle to work through mathematical concepts, but once they thoroughly understand a concept, they build a strong foundation that allows them to file and catalog the information so they can recall and apply it later. Our goal in developing this book is to help students build a strong foundational framework in mathematics that they can readily access and apply to various real-life situations.

How to Use This Book

Students can work on the activities in this book independently, with a partner, or in small groups. The activities build on concepts and skills that you have already taught, but they offer opportunities to expand students' understanding in various ways—from investigating through the use of manipulatives to exploring through representational drawings. What makes the problems in this book unique is that there is no one correct answer for most of them. This allows students to make and share a variety of math problems and solutions using the same activity page. Encourage students to describe their answers using mathematical language—an important part of today's rigorous standards that is often overlooked in math instruction.

Some activities require the use of a spinner, which is printed on the page. To use the spinner, have students place a paper clip on the spinner and use a pencil to hold one end of the clip in place at the center of the spinner. Then, flick a finger to make the paper clip spin.

Each activity comes with an Investigate section, which challenges advanced learners to solve difficult problems or to investigate new concepts at a higher level. Also on every page is a section entitled Write About It (see below). Through writing, students boost long-term memory as they begin to see patterns and better understand how the new concepts relate to their overall understanding of mathematics. After students have completed the writing activity, invite them to share and discuss their responses with a classmate. This provides another essential way for students to reflect on what they have learned, to refine their thinking, and to make connections.

Formative Assessment Ideas

Formative assessments are a great way to evaluate students' strengths and weaknesses. Here are some quick and easy formative assessment ideas.

Write About It: In the Write About It section on each page, students reflect on what they have learned in the activity. For example, students may write the definition of a term in their own words, describe the steps taken to solve a problem, or describe one of the most important concepts learned from the lesson. These written responses help students synthesize what they learned and often provide a quick way to gauge their understanding.

Self-Assessment: After students finish a lesson, ask them to describe their level of understanding of the topic by writing a single word, phrase, or emoji at the top of the page, followed by a one-sentence explanation. For example: "Got It," "Still Trying," "Need Help," or "☺," "☹." Using this technique will not only help you evaluate student comprehension, but it also provides students with an opportunity to reflect and assess their own understanding.

Pair and Share: Provide a conversation prompt and pair up students to discuss. This can provide you with another assessment tool as you circulate around the room listening to conversations. Here are a few prompts to get started:

What is one important idea you want to remember from this lesson? Why do you think it is important?

What was the most difficult part of this lesson and why?

What is one question you have about the lesson today?

As students work through the activities in this book, encourage them to investigate deeply, ask hard questions, and share what they are learning. We hope that they will discover that mathematics is so much more than memorizing algorithms and getting right answers. It is in fact about curiosity, investigation, making connections, and having loads of fun!

Math Standards Correlations

The activities in this book meet the following core standards in mathematics.

OPERATIONS & ALGEBRAIC THINKING

OA.A.1 Interpret a multiplication equation as a comparison, e.g., interpret $35 = 5 \times 7$ as a statement that 35 is 5 times as many as 7 and 7 times as many as 5.

OA.A.2 Multiply or divide to solve word problems involving multiplicative comparison.

OA.A.3 Solve multistep word problems posed with whole numbers and having whole-number answers using the four operations, including problems in which remainders must be interpreted.

OA.B.4 Find all factor pairs for a whole number in the range of 1–100. Recognize that a whole number is a multiple of each of its factors.

OA.C.5 Generate a number or shape pattern that follows a given rule.

NUMBER & OPERATIONS IN BASE TEN

NBT.A.1 Recognize that in a multi-digit whole number, a digit in one place represents ten times what it represents in the place to its right.

NBT.A.2 Read and write multi-digit whole numbers using base-ten numerals, number names, and expanded form. Compare two multi-digit numbers based on meanings of the digits in each place, using >, =, and < symbols to record the results of the comparisons.

NBT.A.3 Use place value understanding to round multi-digit whole numbers to any place.

NBT.B.4 Fluently add and subtract multi-digit whole numbers using the standard algorithm.

NBT.B.5 Multiply a whole number of up to four digits by a one-digit whole number, and multiply two two-digit numbers, using strategies based on place value and the properties of operations.

NBT.B.6 Find whole-number quotients and remainders with up to four-digit dividends and one-digit divisors, using strategies based on place value, the properties of operations, and/or the relationship between multiplication and division.

NUMBER & OPERATIONS: FRACTIONS

NF.A.1 Explain why a fraction a/b is equivalent to a fraction $(n \times a)/(n \times b)$ by using visual fraction models.

NF.A.2 Compare two fractions with different numerators and different denominators, e.g., by creating common denominators or numerators, or by comparing to a benchmark fraction such as 1/2.

NF.B.3 Understand a fraction a/b with $a > 1$ as a sum of fractions $1/b$.

NF.B.4 Apply and extend previous understandings of multiplication to multiply a fraction by a whole number.

NF.C.5 Express a fraction with denominator 10 as an equivalent fraction with denominator 100, and use this technique to add two fractions with respective denominators 10 and 100.

NF.C.6 Use decimal notation for fractions with denominators 10 or 100.

NF.C.7 Compare two decimals to hundredths by reasoning about their size. Recognize that comparisons are valid only when the two decimals refer to the same whole.

MEASUREMENT & DATA

MD.A.1 Know relative sizes of measurement units within one system of units including km, m, cm; kg, g; lb, oz.

MD.A.2 Use the four operations to solve word problems involving distances, liquid volumes, masses of objects.

MD.A.3 Apply the area and perimeter formulas for rectangles in real world and mathematical problems.

MD.B.4 Make a line plot to display a data set of measurements in fractions of a unit (1/2, 1/4, 1/8). Solve problems involving addition and subtraction of fractions by using information presented in line plots.

MD.C.5 Recognize angles as geometric shapes that are formed wherever two rays share a common endpoint and understand concepts of angle measurement.

MD.C.6 Measure angles in whole-number degrees using a protractor. Sketch angles of specified measure.

MD.C.7 Recognize angle measure as additive. When an angle is decomposed into non-overlapping parts, the angle measure of the whole is the sum of the angle measures of the parts.

GEOMETRY

G.A.1 Draw points, lines, line segments, rays, angles (right, acute, obtuse).

G.A.2 Classify two-dimensional figures based on the presence or absence of parallel or perpendicular lines, or the presence or absence of angles of a specified size.

G.A.3 Recognize a line of symmetry for a two-dimensional figure as a line across the figure such that the figure can be folded along the line into matching parts.

#1 Name: _____

Interpret comparison statements as multiplication equations.

Comparison Statements

48 pounds is 12 times as heavy as 4 pounds.

60 inches is 10 times the length of 6 inches.

12 hours is 4 times longer than 3 hours.

24 eggs is 6 times as many as 4 eggs.

9 cups is 3 times as many as 3 cups.

6 feet is 2 times the height of 3 feet.

Choose a comparison statement above. Draw a model, then write an equation.
Complete the table.

Comparison Statement	Draw a Model	Equation
Example: 8 is 4 times as many as 2.	[model: box labeled 2; row of four boxes labeled 1, 2, 3, 4 totaling 8]	4 × 2 = 8

 Investigate: Look at the comparison statement in the example problem above. How can you tell that this statement involves multiplication? Write your own multiplication comparison statement.

 Write About It: On the back of the page, write about how 4 × 2 and 2 × 4 are the same. How are they different?

#2 Name: _____

Interpret comparison statements as multiplication equations.

Use the information below to fill in the blanks. Then, place the correct factor in the box to make each statement true. Finally, show the comparison statement as an equation. The first one has been done for you.

Snowshoe Rabbit	Black Lemur	Striped Skunk	Gray Fox
2 pounds	3 pounds	4 pounds	5 pounds

Raccoon	Jungle Cat	Chinese Water Deer	Swamp Wallaby
6 pounds	10 pounds	12 pounds	15 pounds

1. The __10__ pound jungle cat is ⬚5⬚ times as heavy as the __2__ pound snowshoe rabbit.

__5__ × __2__ = __10__

2. The _____ pound raccoon is ⬚ ⬚ times as heavy as the _____ pound black lemur.

_____ × _____ = _____

3. The _____ pound swamp wallaby is ⬚ ⬚ times as heavy as the _____ pound gray fox.

_____ × _____ = _____

4. The _____ pound Chinese water deer is ⬚ ⬚ times as heavy as the _____ pound striped skunk.

_____ × _____ = _____

🔍 **Investigate:** Write a comparison statement about the weight of two mammals in the chart above. Then, write a matching equation.

✏️ **Write About It:** On the back of the page, use your own words to define the term *equation*.

#3

Name: _____

Multiply or divide to solve word problems involving multiplicative comparison.

Ebony walked 2 times as far as Nia. If Ebony walked 10 miles, how far did Nia walk?

Tape Diagram

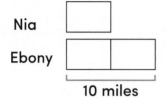

Nia

Ebony

10 miles

If Ebony walked 10 miles and it is 2 times as far as Nia, we need to divide 10 by 2 to find the amount represented in each box.

We can interpret this type of comparison word problem as multiplication or division.

$? \times 2 = 10$ OR $10 \div 2 = ?$

Solution: Nia walked 5 miles.

Choose two comparison word problems below. On the back of the page, draw a tape diagram to solve each problem. Then, write the problem as a multiplication or division equation.

1. Emma sold 4 times more cookies than Paul. If Emma sold 20 cookies, how many did Paul sell?	**2.** At the movie theater, popcorn costs $4 and gummies cost $1. How many times more does popcorn cost than gummies?
3. Antonio has 3 cows on his farm. Jarrod has 12 cows. How many times more cows does Jarrod have than Antonio?	**4.** Walker gathered 18 eggs from his chickens one morning. Walker gathered 3 times more eggs than Stewart gathered. How many eggs did Stewart gather?

 Investigate: Besides tape diagrams, what other tools could you use to help solve comparison word problems (for example, drawing a picture or using counters)? Solve another word problem. This time use a different tool besides a tape diagram. Use the back of the page to show your work.

 Write About It: On the back of the page, write about one question you had during this activity. Did you find the answer?

#**4** Name: _____

Multiply or divide to solve word problems involving multiplicative comparison.

1. Jerome's farm has many animals. Use the clues below to figure out how many animals of each type are on his farm. Complete the table.

Jerome's Farm Animals

Cows	Pigs	Chickens	Horses	Dogs	Cats

- Jerome has 4 times as many cows as horses.

- There are 4 times as many chickens as dogs.

- The chickens laid 24 eggs in two days.
  There are 2 times as many eggs as chickens.

- Jerome has 2 horses on his farm. He has 3 times as many pigs as horses.

- There is one more cat on the farm than dogs.

2. Write your own farm clue statements. Swap with a classmate and solve.

Jerome's Garden Plants

Corn	Carrots	Beans

- Jerome has _____ times as many corn plants as carrot plants.

- Jerome has _____ carrot plants.

- There are _____ more bean plants than carrot plants.

 Investigate: Notice that there are two types of clue statements. Some statements ask you to multiply to find the clue, while others ask you to add. Write one of each type on the back of the page. Then, write your own multiplicative comparison statement and additive comparison statement.

 Write About It: On the back of the page, explain the process you used to solve the first problem on the page.

Write and solve multistep word problems using the four operations.

1. Write your own word problem that requires more than one step to solve. Here's how:

   a. Decide on a theme for your word problem. _____

   b. Decide on the two operations that will be used to find the solution.

   _____

   c. Write your word problem.

   _____

   _____

   _____

   d. Draw a picture.

   _____
   | |
   | |
   | |
   | |
   | |
   | |
   |_____|

   e. Write the solution on a separate sheet of paper. Check to make sure your answer is reasonable.

   f. Swap worksheets with a classmate and solve.

   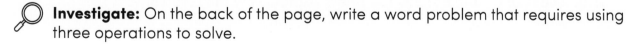 **Investigate:** On the back of the page, write a word problem that requires using three operations to solve.

   Write About It: On the back of the page, give an example from everyday life when you need to use more than one operation to solve a problem.

#6 Name: _____

Write and solve multistep word problems in which remainders must be interpreted.

The **remainder** is the amount left over after dividing.

Three Ways to Interpret Remainders

Write the Remainder as a Fraction	Use Only the Quotient	Add 1 to the Quotient
Rocco has a coil of wire that is 93 inches long. He cuts off 10 inches. If he divides the remaining wire into 9 equal pieces, how long will each piece be?	Asia has a piece of string 93 inches long. She cuts off 10 inches. She wants to divide the remaining string into 9-inch pieces. How many 9-inch pieces of string will Asia have?	Ben had 93 marbles. He gave away 10. Now he wants to put the remaining marbles into small bags. Each bag holds 9 marbles. How many bags will Ben need?
$$\begin{array}{r} 9\,r\,2 \\ 9\overline{|8\ 3} \\ -8\ 1 \\ \hline 2 \end{array}$$	$$\begin{array}{r} 9\,r\,2 \\ 9\overline{|8\ 3} \\ -8\ 1 \\ \hline 2 \end{array}$$	$$\begin{array}{r} 9\,r\,2 \\ 9\overline{|8\ 3} \\ -8\ 1 \\ \hline 2 \end{array}$$
Answer: The length of each piece of wire is $9\frac{2}{9}$ inches. (The remainder 2 inches can be divided into 9 equal pieces.)	**Answer:** Asia will have 9 9-inch pieces of string. (We drop the remainder.)	**Answer:** Ben will need 10 bags in all. 9 bags will have 9 marbles and 1 bag will have the remaining 2 marbles.

Write a two-step division word problem with a remainder. Swap with a classmate and solve.

_____

_____

_____

 Investigate: Create another two-step division word problem. Make sure the remainder is interpreted in a different way than in your first word problem. Swap with a classmate and solve.

 Write About It: On the back of the page, explain why the remainder must be less than the divisor.

Investigate Math: Grade 4 © Cindi Mitchell, Scholastic Inc.

Identify factor pairs and multiples.

✓ **You will need:** counters

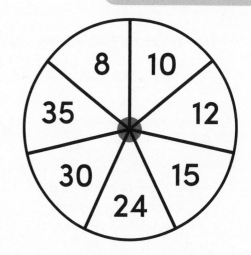

A **factor pair** is a set of two numbers we multiply to get a product. For example, 2 and 4 is a factor pair for 8.

Multiples are products of any given whole number and another whole number. For example, the first four multiples of 4 are 4, 8, 12, and 16.

Spin the spinner to get a number. Write it in the first column. Grab that number of counters to make arrays that show all of its factor pairs. Draw the arrays below, then list all of the factor pairs. Finally, list the first four multiples of the number.

Number	Arrays	Factor Pairs	Multiples
Example: 6	●●● ●●● 2 × 3 = 6 ●●●●●● 1 × 6 = 6	2, 3 1, 6	6, 12, 18, 24

🔍 **Investigate:** Some numbers have factor pairs that are the same number. For instance, 2, 2 is a factor pair for 4. Can you give more examples?

✏️ **Write About It:** On the back of the page, define the terms *factor* and *multiple* in your own words.

#8 Name: _____

Identify prime and composite numbers.

✓ **You will need:** counters

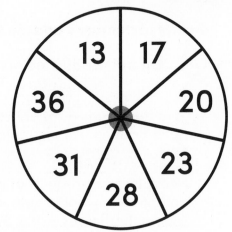

A **prime number** is a number greater than 1 that has 1 and itself as its only factors. (For example: 2, 5, 13, and 19)

A **composite number** is a number greater than 1 that has more than one factor pair. (For example: 4, 6, 9, and 12)

Spin the spinner to get a number and write it in the first column. Grab that number of counters to make arrays that show all of its factor pairs. Draw the arrays below, then list all of the factor pairs. Finally, write whether the number is prime or composite.

Number	Arrays	Factor Pairs	Prime or Composite
Example: 11	● ● ● ● ● ● ● ● ● ● ● 1 × 11 = 11	1, 11	prime

 Investigate: Choose a number and keep it secret. Write clues that will help a classmate to identify it. Use words such as *prime*, *composite*, *factors*, and *multiples*. Swap with a classmate and solve.

Example: The mystery number is a composite number. The number is greater than 10 and less than 20. It is an odd number, and one of its multiples is 30.
[**Answer:** The mystery number is 15.]

 Write About It: On the back of the page, define the terms *prime* and *composite* in your own words.

Generate number patterns that follow a rule and identify different features.

Choose a pattern rule below. Note the first term in the pattern. Write the information in the first column. Then, write the first ten numbers in the pattern. Finally, identify different features. For example: Are there odd or even number patterns? Is there a pattern in the ones place? Do you notice other interesting features in the numbers?

Pattern Rules		
Add 2.	**Multiply by 2.**	**Add 5.**
The first term is 1.	The first term is 2.	The first term is 15.
Subtract 10.	**Multiply by 3.**	**Add 4.**
The first term is 190.	The first term is 1.	The first term is 4.

A **pattern** is an ordered set of numbers or objects arranged according to a rule. Each number in a sequence is called a **term**.

Pattern Rule	Number Pattern	Identify Features
Example: Add 5. The first term is 5.	5, 10, 15, 20, 25, 30, 35, 40, 45, 50	The numbers alternate between odd and even. The pattern in the ones place is: 5, 0, 5, 0. The pattern is increasing.

 Investigate: On the back of the page, generate a pattern. Write a rule for your pattern and identify the first term. Swap patterns with a classmate and continue each other's pattern.

 Write About It: On the back of the page, write about some of the things you noticed when you extended the number patterns.

#10 Name: _____

Generate shape patterns that follow a rule and identify different features.

Choose a shape pattern below and draw a picture in the first column. Identify what shape comes next. Finally, identify features in the pattern. For example: How do you know what shape comes next? What number pattern matches the shape pattern? Are there odd or even number patterns? Are there other interesting features?

Shape Patterns

· ∴ ∷	:: ⣿ ⣿	⊟ ⊞ ⊞
△ ◇ ⬠	▭ ▭ ▭	⌐ ⌐ ⌐

> A **pattern** is an ordered set of numbers or objects arranged according to a rule.

Copy the Pattern	What Comes Next?	Identify Features
Example: ▯ ⊞ ⊞	⊞⊞⊞	I know what comes next because the pattern doubles by adding columns of 2 blocks. The number pattern is 2, 4, 8, 16, 32, 64. All of the numbers are even. The pattern is increasing.

 Investigate: On the back of the page, generate a shape pattern. Draw the next three shapes in the pattern. Then, swap shape patterns with a classmate and continue each other's pattern.

 Write About It: On the back of the page, write about some of the things you noticed when you extended the shape pattern.

#11 Name: _____

Recognize the value of digits in multi-digit numbers.

 You will need (for each small group): 2 copies of Place Value Blocks (page 18)
• clear tape • scissors

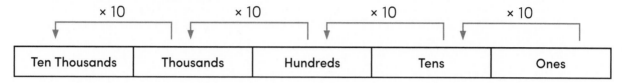

	× 10		× 10		× 10		× 10	
Ten Thousands		Thousands		Hundreds		Tens		Ones

1. Look at the place-value chart above. What pattern do you see as you move from right to left?

_____

_____

2. Working in small groups, cut out Place Value Blocks as directed below:

• To model the number 1, cut out a single block.

• To model 10, cut out a strip of 10 blocks.

• To model 100, cut out a grid of 100 blocks.

• To model 1,000 and 10,000, cut out and tape together 100 blocks end to end.

3. Place the models in order from least to greatest. Then, answer these questions.

• How many single blocks does it take to model 10? _____

• How many strips of 10 does it take to model 100? _____

• How many 100 blocks did you need to model 1,000? _____

• How many 1,000 blocks did you need to model 10,000? _____

• Describe the pattern you notice as the models increase in size.

_____

_____

 Investigate: How many 100 blocks would you need to model 100,000? Explain how you got the answer.

Write About It: Look at the number 9,349. Compare the values of the digit in the thousands place and the digit in the ones place.

Place Value Blocks

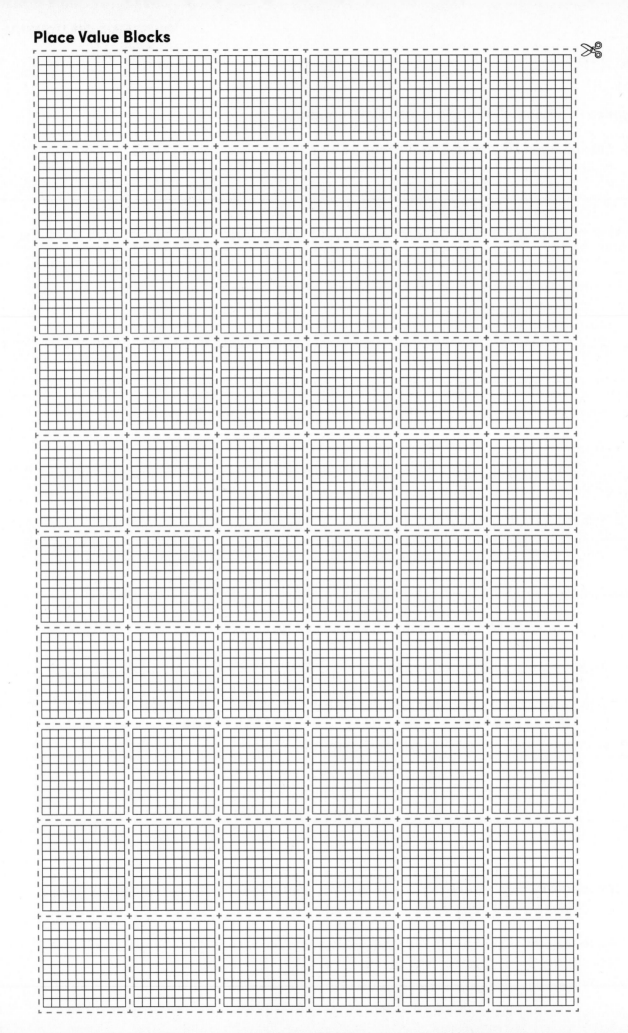

Investigate Math: Grade 4 © Cindi Mitchell, Scholastic Inc.

#12 Name: _____

Recognize the value of digits in multi-digit numbers.

✓ **You will need:** number cube

1. Roll the number cube five times. Write the five-digit number in the first column. Then, find the value of the digit with the bold underline.

Example:	
<u>**3**</u> 4 , 2 1 2	30,000
___ ___ , **___** ___ ___	
___ ___ , ___ **___** ___	
___ ___ , ___ **___** ___	

2. Roll the number cube six times. Write the six-digit number in the first column. Scramble the digits and write a different six-digit number in the second column. Choose a digit that is the same in both numbers. Circle each. Compare their values.

Example:	
4 2 1 , 6 ① 4	6 4 4 , 1 2 ①
The value of the 1 in the tens place is 10 times more than the 1 in the ones place.	
___ ___ ___ , ___ ___ ___	___ ___ ___ , ___ ___ ___
___ ___ ___ , ___ ___ ___	___ ___ ___ , ___ ___ ___

 Investigate: Build a six-digit number with base-ten blocks on your desk. Draw a picture. Swap pictures with a classmate and identify each other's number.

 Write About It: On the back of the page, write about the most important thing you learned in this lesson.

#13 Name: _____

Read and write multi-digit numbers.

✓ **You will need:** number cube

Roll the number cube six times. Write the six-digit number in the place-value chart. Then, record the number in standard form, word form, and expanded form.

Example:

Hundred Thousands	Ten Thousands	Thousands	Hundreds	Tens	Ones
4	5	6	1	4	2

Standard Form: 456,142

Word Form: four hundred fifty-six thousand one hundred forty-two

Expanded Form: 400,000 + 50,000 + 6,000 + 100 + 40 + 2

Hundred Thousands	Ten Thousands	Thousands	Hundreds	Tens	Ones

Standard Form:

Word Form:

Expanded Form:

Hundred Thousands	Ten Thousands	Thousands	Hundreds	Tens	Ones

Standard Form:

Word Form:

Expanded Form:

 Investigate: Write a six-digit number on a piece of paper but keep it secret. Write a list of clues that could be used to identify the number. Swap clues with a classmate and solve each other's mystery number.

 Write About It: Joan wrote 45,261 in word form as "forty-five thousand and two hundred sixty-one." Pablo wrote "forty-five thousand two hundred sixty-one." Who wrote the number correctly? Explain.

Investigate Math: Grade 4 © Cindi Mitchell, Scholastic Inc.

#14 **Name:** _____

Compare multi-digit numbers.

 You will need: 8 index cards • pencil • Less Than, Greater Than game sheet
(page 22) • number cube

Players: 2

Before You Play

To make comparison cards, write "<" on four index cards and ">" on the other four cards.

Play "Less Than, Greater Than"

1. Shuffle the comparison cards and stack them facedown. Give players a copy of the
"Less Than, Greater Than" game sheet.

2. For each round, players take turns rolling a number cube five times and filling in the
digits on the game sheet. Players may fill in the digits in any order.

3. Both players read their numbers aloud. To find out who wins the round, one player turns
over an index card. If the card shows <, the player with the lower number gets one point.
If the card shows >, the player with the higher number gets one point. Return the card to
the bottom of the stack.

4. Play four rounds. The player with the most points at the end wins.

Investigate: What hints would you give someone to help them win the game "Less
Than, Greater Than"?

Write About It: On the back of the page, describe the process you use to compare
numbers.

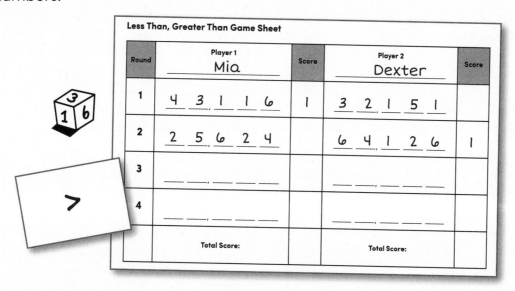

Less Than, Greater Than Game Sheet

Round	Player 1 Mia	Score	Player 2 Dexter	Score
1	4 3 1 , 1 6	1	3 2 , 1 5 1	
2	2 5 , 6 2 4		6 4 1 2 6	1
3	___ ___ , ___ ___ ___		___ ___ , ___ ___ ___	
4	___ ___ , ___ ___ ___		___ ___ , ___ ___ ___	
	Total Score:		Total Score:	

Less Than, Greater Than Game Sheet

Round	Player 1 _____	Score	Player 2 _____	Score
1	____ ____, ____ ____ ____		____ ____, ____ ____ ____	
2	____ ____, ____ ____ ____		____ ____, ____ ____ ____	
3	____ ____, ____ ____ ____		____ ____, ____ ____ ____	
4	____ ____, ____ ____ ____		____ ____, ____ ____ ____	
	Total Score:		**Total Score:**	

Investigate Math: Grade 4 © Cindi Mitchell, Scholastic Inc.

- -

Less Than, Greater Than Game Sheet

Round	Player 1 _____	Score	Player 2 _____	Score
1	____ ____, ____ ____ ____		____ ____, ____ ____ ____	
2	____ ____, ____ ____ ____		____ ____, ____ ____ ____	
3	____ ____, ____ ____ ____		____ ____, ____ ____ ____	
4	____ ____, ____ ____ ____		____ ____, ____ ____ ____	
	Total Score:		**Total Score:**	

Investigate Math: Grade 4 © Cindi Mitchell, Scholastic Inc.

Round multi-digit whole numbers.

The state of Idaho is expecting to receive 82,299 doses of vaccine. To the nearest ten thousand, how many doses is Idaho expecting to receive?

We can use a number line to help round numbers like 82,299 to the nearest ten thousand.

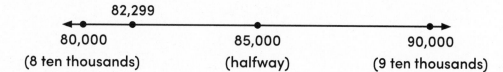

82,299 is closer to 80,000 than to 90,000. 82,299 rounded to the nearest ten thousand is 80,000. Idaho is expecting to receive about 80,000 doses of vaccine.

1. Imagine that you are a teacher. Choose one of the numbers in the box. Show how to round the number to the nearest ten thousand in each of the following ways:

12,789	285,321	75,000	54,001
322,400	67,213	18,536	57,903

• Write a step-by-step explanation about how to round the number.

• Create a number line to show your thinking.

• Give a word problem example.

2. Share the information with a classmate or small group.

🔍 **Investigate:** On the back of the page, write five numbers that round to 20,000.

✏️ **Write About It:** On the back of the page, give examples of when you might use rounding to solve everyday problems.

#16 Name: _____

Round multi-digit whole numbers.

✓ **You will need:** number cube

In 2020 the population in St. Petersburg, Florida, was 244,769. What is the population to the nearest hundred thousand?

244,769

←————•————————••————————————•————→
200,000   250,000   300,000
                 (halfway)

244,769 is closer to 200,000 than to 300,000. The 2020 population in St. Petersburg to the nearest hundred thousand is 200,000.

Roll a number cube to fill in each space with a digit. Round each number you created to the nearest hundred thousand. Explain how you got your answer.

Number	Round Number to Nearest Hundred Thousand
____ ____ ____, ____ ____ ____	
Explain how you got your answer.	
____ ____ ____, ____ ____ ____	
Explain how you got your answer.	
____ ____ ____, ____ ____ ____	
Explain how you got your answer.	

🔍 **Investigate:** Rose rounds the number 3,992,199 to the nearest ten thousand. Her answer is 4,000,000. Is she correct? Explain.

✏️ **Write About It:** What is the purpose of rounding numbers? Write your answer on the back of the page.

Investigate Math: Grade 4 © Cindi Mitchell, Scholastic Inc.

#17 Name: _____

Add multi-digit whole numbers using the standard algorithm.

✓ **You will need:** number cube

> When adding large numbers, it is helpful to use a grid to make sure that the numbers are lined up correctly.
>
> | | 1 | | 1 | | | 1 | |
> |---|---|---|---|---|---|---|---|
> | | 1 | 0 | 2, | 3 | 8 | 8 |
> | + | 1 | 5 | 9, | 7 | 0 | 9 |
> | | 2 | 6 | 2, | 0 | 9 | 7 |

Roll a number cube to fill in each shaded block with a digit. Then, find the sum.

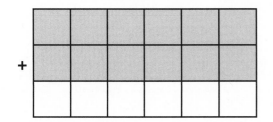
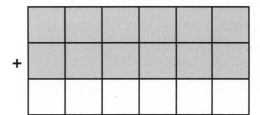

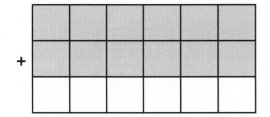
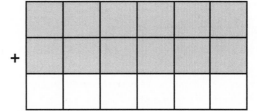

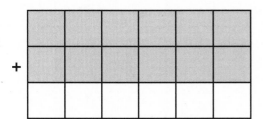
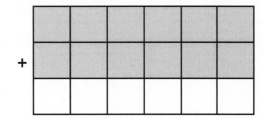

 Investigate: Write a word problem to go along with one of the problems you solved.

 Write About It: What advice would you give someone who is just beginning to learn how to find the sum of larger multi-digit numbers? Write your advice on the back of the page.

#18 Name: _____

Subtract multi-digit whole numbers using the standard algorithm.

✓ **You will need:** number cube

When subtracting large numbers, it is helpful to use a grid to make sure that the numbers are lined up correctly.

					5	14
9	7	3,	7	~~6~~	~~4~~
− 7	3	1,	5	4	5
2	4	2,	2	1	9

Roll the number cube six times to create a 6-digit number. Repeat to create another 6-digit number. Write the numbers in the shaded blocks. Make sure the larger number is in the top row and the smaller number is in the bottom row. Find the difference.

____ ____ ____ , ____ ____ ____   ____ ____ ____ , ____ ____ ____

____ ____ ____ , ____ ____ ____   ____ ____ ____ , ____ ____ ____

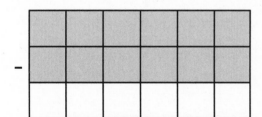

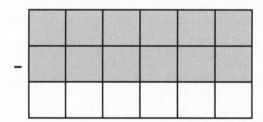

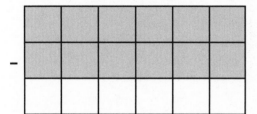

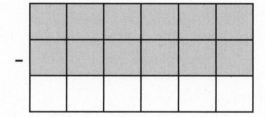

🔍 **Investigate:** Write a word problem to go along with one of the problems you solved.

✏️ **Write About It:** What advice would you give to someone about how to subtract across zeros in a problem like this: 500 − 317? Write your advice on the back of the page.

26

#19   Name: _____

Multiply three-digit numbers by one-digit numbers.

✓ **You will need:** Factor Fun game sheet (page 28) • 2 number cubes • base-ten blocks

Players: 2

Play "Factor Fun"

1. For each round, players take turns rolling a number cube to fill in the digits on the game sheet. Players may fill in the digits in the multiplication expression in any order.

2. To find the product, players model their multiplication expression using base-ten blocks. (See example below.)

3. The player with the larger product wins the round and gets one point.

4. Play continues for four rounds. The player with the most points at the end of the game wins.

Example: $2 \times 136 = ?$

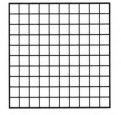 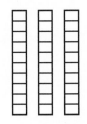 

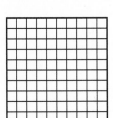 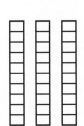 

| 2 hundreds = 200 | 6 tens = 60
Move 1 ten here = 70 ⟵ | 12 ones = 1 ten and 2 ones
Leave 2 ones. |

The product is 272.

🔍 **Investigate:** What is the largest possible product someone could have when playing the game? What is the smallest?

✏️ **Write About It:** On the back of the page, describe a strategy you used to help win the game.

Factor Fun Game Sheet

Round	Player 1 _____	Score	Player 2 _____	Score
1	_____ × _____ _____ _____ =		_____ × _____ _____ _____ =	
2	_____ × _____ _____ _____ =		_____ × _____ _____ _____ =	
3	_____ × _____ _____ _____ =		_____ × _____ _____ _____ =	
4	_____ × _____ _____ _____ =		_____ × _____ _____ _____ =	
	Total Score:		**Total Score:**	

Factor Fun Game Sheet

Round	Player 1 _____	Score	Player 2 _____	Score
1	_____ × _____ _____ _____ =		_____ × _____ _____ _____ =	
2	_____ × _____ _____ _____ =		_____ × _____ _____ _____ =	
3	_____ × _____ _____ _____ =		_____ × _____ _____ _____ =	
4	_____ × _____ _____ _____ =		_____ × _____ _____ _____ =	
	Total Score:		**Total Score:**	

#20

Name: _____

Multiply two 2-digit numbers.

✓ **You will need:** grid paper

We can use area models to find the product of two 2-digit numbers, like 15 × 18. Here's how:

- Draw the outline of a 15 × 18 rectangle on grid paper.

- Break apart the factors into tens and ones and show smaller rectangles. Color each part.

- Find the area of each rectangle.

  A: 10 × 10 = 100   B: 10 × 8 = 80

  C: 5 × 10 = 50   D: 5 × 8 = 40

- Find the sum of the partial products.

  100 + 80 + 50 + 40 = 270

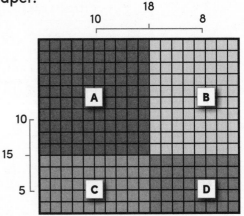

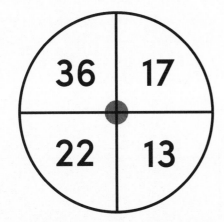

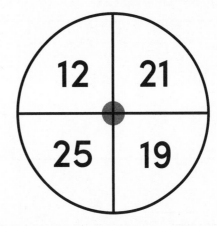

Spin both spinners to create a multiplication expression. On a sheet of grid paper, represent the expression as an area model. Be sure to follow the steps above and provide answers for each step. Share your model with a classmate.

 Investigate: Identify the missing numbers. What multiplication expression does the model represent? Find the product.

	20	?
10	200	50
?	80	20

_____ × _____ = _____

 Write About It: On the back of the page, explain how to break apart 2-digit factors into tens and ones.

Investigate Math: Grade 4 © Cindi Mitchell, Scholastic Inc.

#21

Name: _____

Divide a whole number by a one-digit whole number.

Make solving division problems simple and easy by using the Distributive Property to break apart the dividend.

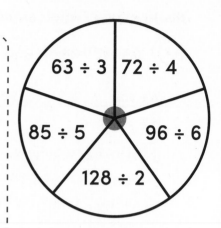

Divide: 108 ÷ 6 ◄ | Think: What addends total the dividend and are compatible with 6?

108 ÷ 6 = (60 ÷ 6) + (48 ÷ 6) ◄ | We can use the addends 60 and 48 because the sum of the addends is 108, and they can both easily be divided by 6.

= 10 + 8 ◄ | Find the sum.

= 18

Spin the spinner to get a division expression. Use the Distributive Property to break apart the dividend and solve. Show your work.

Investigate: Use another method you have learned to solve the division problem above. Which method do you like best and why?

Write About It: On the back of the page, write about a real-life problem that can be solved using the Distributive Property.

Investigate Math: Grade 4 © Cindi Mitchell, Scholastic Inc.

Divide a whole number by a one-digit whole number.

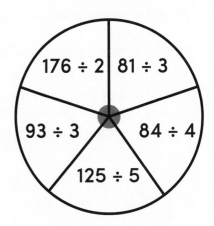

✓ **You will need:** base-ten blocks

- -

We can use base-ten blocks to model a division problem.

Divide: 45 ÷ 3

a. Model 45 with base-ten blocks. (You can also draw stick figures to represent rods and ones.)

b. Draw three boxes. Start by placing a ten in each box. There is one ten left over, so regroup it into ones. Now we have 15 ones.

c. Next, share the 15 ones evenly into the three boxes.

45 ÷ 3 = (30 ÷ 3) + (15 ÷ 3) = 10 + 5 = 15

- -

1. Spin the spinner to get a division expression.
Use base-ten blocks to solve.
Draw a picture to model your solution.

2. Swap the model of your solution with a classmate. Can he or she identify which division problem you solved?

 Investigate: Use another method you have learned to solve your division problem. After using both methods, explain which method you like better and why.

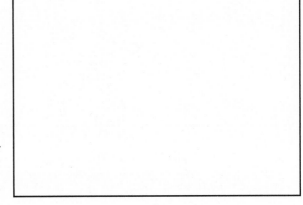

 Write About It: On the back of the page, write a division problem and solve it using base-ten blocks. Then, tell how you solved the problem.

#23 Name: _____

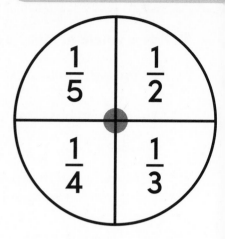

Recognize and generate equivalent fractions.

✓ **You will need:** fraction tiles

> **Equivalent fractions** represent the same part of the whole,
> but they have different numerators and denominators.
> We can use fraction tiles to find equivalent fractions.

1											
$\frac{1}{6}$		$\frac{1}{6}$		$\frac{1}{6}$		$\frac{1}{6}$		$\frac{1}{6}$		$\frac{1}{6}$	
$\frac{1}{12}$	$\frac{1}{12}$	$\frac{1}{12}$	$\frac{1}{12}$	$\frac{1}{12}$	$\frac{1}{12}$	$\frac{1}{12}$	$\frac{1}{12}$	$\frac{1}{12}$	$\frac{1}{12}$	$\frac{1}{12}$	$\frac{1}{12}$

$$\frac{2}{6} = \frac{4}{12}$$

1. Spin the spinner to get a fraction.
   Use fraction tiles to find an equivalent fraction. Draw a picture.

2. Repeat step 1 to work on a different fraction.

 Investigate: Look at the fraction tiles. Identify all of the fractions that are equivalent to $\frac{1}{2}$. What do you notice about the relationship between the numerators and denominators?

 Write About It: On the back of the page, define the term *equivalent fraction* in your own words.

 **Name:** _____

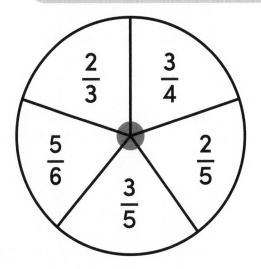

Recognize and generate equivalent fractions.

 You will need: fraction tiles

To find an equivalent fraction, multiply both the numerator and denominator by a fraction equivalent to 1.

$$\frac{1}{2} = \frac{1}{2} \times \frac{2}{2} = \frac{2}{4} \qquad \frac{1}{2} \text{ is equivalent to } \frac{2}{4}$$

A fraction that has the same numerator and denominator is equivalent to 1. $\frac{2}{2}$ is equivalent to 1.

Spin the spinner. Write the fraction in the first column. Find an equivalent fraction using fraction tiles on your desk. Then, draw a picture. Next, use multiplication to show the same equivalent fraction. Finally, write the equivalent fraction. Repeat using different fractions.

Fraction	Fraction Tiles	Multiplication	Equivalent Fraction
Example: $\frac{1}{2}$	(1) — shaded diagram showing $\frac{1}{2}$, $\frac{1}{2}$ and $\frac{1}{4}$, $\frac{1}{4}$, $\frac{1}{4}$, $\frac{1}{4}$	$\frac{1}{2} \times \frac{2}{2} = \frac{2}{4}$	$\frac{2}{4}$

 Investigate: Look at the fraction tiles. Find a fraction that is equivalent to $\frac{2}{3}$. Find a fraction that is not equivalent to $\frac{2}{3}$. Explain how you know when two fractions are equivalent.

 Write About It: Look at the fraction tiles. Name eight fractions that are equivalent to 1. Explain how you know when a fraction is equivalent to 1.

Compare fractional parts represented by the same fraction.

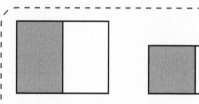

Sometimes $\frac{1}{2}$ of one rectangle is smaller or larger than $\frac{1}{2}$ of another rectangle.

Read each statement. Decide if it is true or false. If the statement is true, give an example. If the statement is false, explain why.

T or **F**   **1.** Sometimes $\frac{1}{2}$ of one rectangle is the same size as $\frac{1}{2}$ of another rectangle.

T or **F**   **2.** Sometimes $\frac{1}{4}$ of one circle is larger than $\frac{1}{4}$ of another circle.

T or **F**   **3.** Sometimes $\frac{1}{4}$ of one cookie is larger than $\frac{1}{2}$ of another cookie.

T or **F**   **4.** If rectangle A is larger than rectangle B, $\frac{1}{2}$ of rectangle A is smaller than $\frac{1}{2}$ of rectangle B.

Investigate: Give an example in which $\frac{1}{2}$ of the people in one group is more than $\frac{1}{4}$ of the people in another group.

Write About It: Do fractional parts always represent the same whole? Explain.

Name: _____

Compare two fractions with different numerators and denominators.

✓ **You will need:** fraction tiles

Compare $\frac{1}{4}$ and $\frac{5}{8}$.

$\frac{1}{4}$ is equivalent to $\frac{2}{8}$. $\frac{1 \times 2}{4 \times 2} = \frac{2}{8}$	The fractions have common denominators. $\frac{2}{8}$ and $\frac{5}{8}$	We compare the numerators. 2 < 5, so $\frac{2}{8} < \frac{5}{8}$

$\frac{1}{8} \bigcirc \frac{1}{4}$	$\frac{2}{3} \bigcirc \frac{5}{6}$	$\frac{2}{5} \bigcirc \frac{1}{10}$	$\frac{1}{3} \bigcirc \frac{3}{4}$	$\frac{5}{6} \bigcirc \frac{8}{12}$	$\frac{1}{2} \bigcirc \frac{4}{8}$

Choose one of the fraction pairs above. Compare the fractions using fraction tiles. Then, draw a picture below. Next, compare fractions by finding a common denominator and comparing numerators. Finally, compare using symbols >, =, <.

Fraction Pair	Use Fraction Tiles		Find Common Denominator	Write <, =, >
Example: $\frac{1}{4}$, $\frac{5}{8}$	1 $\frac{1}{4}$ $\frac{1}{4}$ $\frac{1}{4}$ $\frac{1}{4}$ $\frac{1}{8}$ $\frac{1}{8}$ $\frac{1}{8}$ $\frac{1}{8}$ $\frac{1}{8}$ $\frac{1}{8}$ $\frac{1}{8}$ $\frac{1}{8}$		$\frac{1}{4} = \frac{2}{8}$ $\frac{2}{8} \bigcirc \frac{5}{8}$	$\frac{2}{8} < \frac{5}{8}$

 Investigate: If the numerators of two fractions are the same, how can you tell which fraction is greater? Use the back of the page to answer the question and give an example.

 Write About It: On the back of the page, explain how you can tell if a fraction is less than or greater than $\frac{1}{2}$. Give examples.

Decompose fractions into a sum of fractions with the same denominator.

✓ **You will need:** fraction tiles

Decompose $\frac{7}{8}$.

To decompose a fraction, break the fraction into smaller fractions with the same denominator.

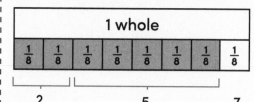

Can you identify other ways to decompose $\frac{7}{8}$?

$$\frac{2}{8} + \frac{5}{8} = \frac{7}{8}$$

1. Choose a fraction: $\frac{3}{4}$, $\frac{4}{8}$, $\frac{3}{10}$, $\frac{4}{12}$.

Use fraction tiles to find two or more ways to decompose the fraction.

Draw examples.

Write an equation.

2. Choose a fraction: $\frac{5}{6}$, $\frac{6}{8}$, $\frac{8}{10}$, $\frac{7}{12}$.

Use fraction tiles to find two or more ways to decompose the fraction.

Draw examples.

Write an equation.

 Investigate: Use fraction tiles to find all of the possible ways to decompose $\frac{4}{5}$. How many ways did you find?

 Write About It: Imagine that you and a friend are sharing a cookie cake divided into four equal sections. On the back of the page, describe all of the possible ways you can share the cookie.

Add and subtract parts of a whole.

✓ **You will need:** fraction tiles

We can use fraction tiles to model addition and subtraction of fractions.

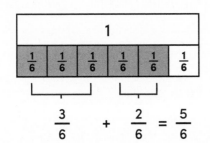

Find the sum: $\frac{3}{6} + \frac{2}{6} =$

$$\frac{3}{6} \quad + \quad \frac{2}{6} = \frac{5}{6}$$

Find the difference: $\frac{5}{6} - \frac{1}{6} =$

$$\frac{5}{6} \quad - \quad \frac{1}{6} = \frac{4}{6}$$

$\frac{1}{4} + \frac{1}{4} =$	$\frac{2}{8} + \frac{2}{8} =$	$\frac{2}{10} + \frac{1}{10} =$	$\frac{7}{8} - \frac{3}{8} =$	$\frac{5}{6} - \frac{1}{6} =$	$\frac{8}{12} - \frac{1}{12} =$

Choose a fraction problem above. Find the sum or difference using fraction tiles on your desk. Draw a picture. Then, write an equation. Repeat to fill in the table.

Draw a Picture	Write an Equation

 Investigate: Look at Allen's solution for the problem at right. Is he correct? Use the back of the page to explain your answer.

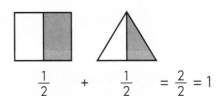

$$\frac{1}{2} \quad + \quad \frac{1}{2} \quad = \frac{2}{2} = 1$$

 Write About It: On the back of the page, create a word problem using the information in one of the fraction problems you solved.

#29 Name: _____

Add and subtract mixed numbers with common denominators.

Mary Ellen's Egg Shop sells flavored candy eggs and packages them in egg cartons. Mary Ellen got the following orders.

$1\frac{4}{12}$ watermelon (W)	$\frac{8}{12}$ marshmallow (M)	$1\frac{11}{12}$ blueberry (B)	$\frac{9}{12}$ strawberry (S)
$1\frac{9}{12}$ marshmallow (M)	$1\frac{7}{12}$ strawberry (S)	$1\frac{7}{12}$ peppermint (P)	$1\frac{7}{12}$ chocolate (C)

Choose an order and write the information in the first column. In the second column, fill the order using the least number of egg cartons. In the third column, identify the total number of egg cartons needed. Finally, write an equation in the last column.

Order Information	Egg Carton Model	# of Cartons	Equation
Example: $1\frac{1}{12}$ Chocolate $1\frac{3}{12}$ Marshmallow		3	$1\frac{1}{12} + 1\frac{3}{12} = 2\frac{4}{12}$

🔍 **Investigate:** Jack bought $4\frac{5}{12}$ cartons of eggs. He gave some eggs to a friend, and he had $3\frac{1}{12}$ left. How much did Jack give away?

✏️ **Write About It:** On the back of the page, give an example of when you might add or subtract mixed numbers in everyday life.

#30 Name: _____

Solve problems involving multiplication of a fraction by a whole number.

Distance From Milo's House

Sports Field . . . . . . $\frac{2}{3}$ mile		Pizza Parlor . . . . . . $\frac{1}{2}$ mile	
School . . . . $\frac{3}{4}$ mile		Drug Store . . . . $\frac{4}{5}$ mile	
Post Office . . . . $\frac{7}{8}$ mile		Grocery Store . . . . . $\frac{1}{4}$ mile	

1. Use the information above to write a word problem involving multiplication of a fraction by a whole number.

_____

_____

_____

2. Draw a model of the problem.

3. Write an equation. _____

4. On the back of the page, write the solution to the problem, along with a detailed explanation of how to solve the problem. Then, swap worksheets with a classmate and solve each other's problem. Compare solutions.

Investigate: If Milo walks to the sports field four times ($4 \times \frac{2}{3}$), does he walk more than or less than four miles? Explain.

Write About It: On the back of the page, explain how you can use repeated addition to solve the word problem you wrote.

#31 Name: _____

Add fractions with denominators of 10 and 100.

Find the sum of $\frac{5}{10} + \frac{20}{100}$.

To add fractions with different denominators, we need to first write the addends as fractions with common denominators.

Write $\frac{5}{10}$ as a fraction with a denominator of 100.

$\frac{5}{10} + \frac{20}{100} =$

$\frac{50}{100} + \frac{20}{100} = \frac{70}{100}$

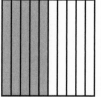

We can see that $\frac{5}{10}$ and $\frac{50}{100}$ are equivalent fractions.

$\frac{1}{10} + \frac{30}{100} =$	$\frac{3}{10} + \frac{40}{100} =$	$\frac{7}{10} + \frac{10}{100} =$	$\frac{4}{10} + \frac{40}{100} =$

1. Choose one of the problems above. Find the sum.

2. Shade the model to show your work.

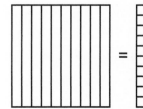 =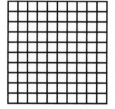

Express the fraction with a denominator of 10 as an equivalent fraction with a denominator of 100.

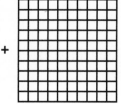 + 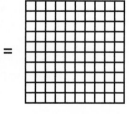 =

Find the sum.

3. Choose another problem above. Find the sum.

 Investigate: Write $\frac{60}{100}$ as an equivalent fraction with a denominator of 10. Explain how you solved the problem.

 Write About It: On the back of the page, explain why $\frac{3}{10}$ is equivalent to $\frac{30}{100}$.

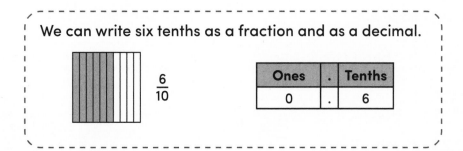

#32 Name: _____

Write tenths in decimal and fraction notations.

We can write six tenths as a fraction and as a decimal.

$\frac{6}{10}$

Ones	.	Tenths
0	.	6

Olivia sewed 10 blocks of fabric together to make a table runner.

Answer each question with both fraction and decimal notation.

1. What part of the table runner has hearts? _____

2. What part of the table runner has a black background? _____

3. What part of the table runner has stripes? _____

🔍 **Investigate:** Fill in the missing fractions and decimals on the number line below. Then, locate and circle the answers to the questions you wrote about the table runner above.

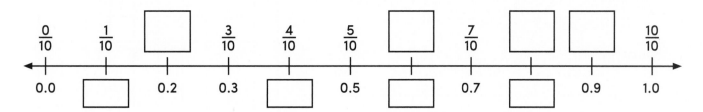

✏️ **Write About It:** On the back of the page, write a definition for the term *decimal* in your own words.

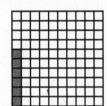

#33 Name: _____

Write hundredths in decimal and fraction notation.

✓ **You will need:** crayons

We can write six hundredths as a fraction and as a decimal.

$\frac{6}{100}$

Ones	.	Tenths	Hundredths
0	.	0	6

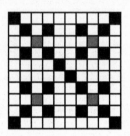

Look at the design on the 100-grid at right. Answer the questions below. Write your answers as a fraction and as a decimal.

1. What part of the design is colored black? _____

2. What part of the design is colored gray? _____

3. Now, color the 100-grid at right to create a design. Use three different crayon colors. Write two questions about your design that require decimal and fraction answers. Write the answers on the back of the page. Swap with a classmate and solve. Compare answers.

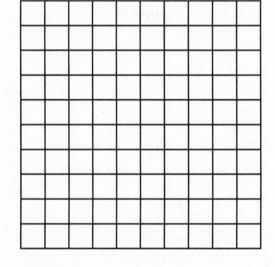

Question 1:

_____

Question 2:

_____

 Investigate: Look at the black-and-white design above. Is it possible to create a different design but still have the same fractional parts of black and gray? Explain.

 Write About It: Are 0.3 and 0.30 equivalent decimals? Use the back of the page to explain.

Investigate Math: Grade 4 © Cindi Mitchell, Scholastic Inc.

#34 Name: _____

Compare decimals to the tenths.

We can compare decimals using a model or a number line.

Compare 0.1 and 0.2.

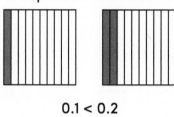

0.1 < 0.2

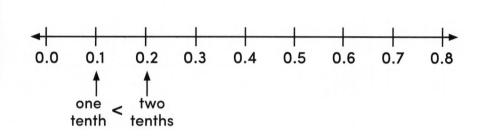

one tenth **<** two tenths

1. Choose two decimals on the number line above. _____

2. Compare the decimals using a model.

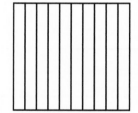 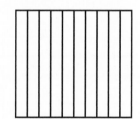

3. Compare the decimals using a number line.

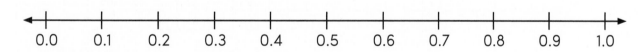

🔍 **Investigate:** Use a model to compare 0.25 and one of the decimals you chose above. Show your work below.

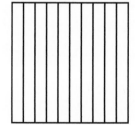 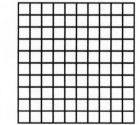

✏️ **Write About It:** On the back of the page, write two decimals that are equivalent. Explain how you know that they are equivalent.

#35 Name: _____

Compare decimals to the hundredths.

We can compare decimals using a model or a number line.

Compare 0.13 and 0.31.

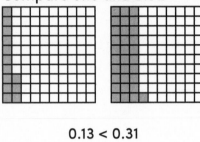

0.13 < 0.31

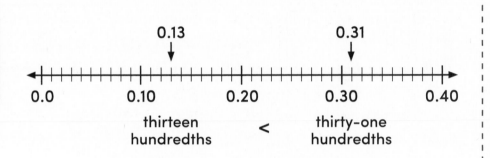

thirteen hundredths **<** thirty-one hundredths

---

1. Choose two decimals on the number line above. _____

2. Compare the decimals using a model.

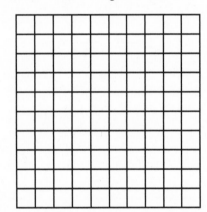
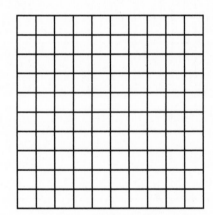

3. Compare the decimals using a number line.

🔍 **Investigate:** Use a number line and a model to compare 0.3 and one of the decimals you chose. (Don't forget: 0.3 and 0.30 are equivalent.)

✏️ **Write About It:** In your own words, define the terms *tenths* and *hundredths*. Compare the size of 1 tenth and 1 hundredth.

Compare relative sizes of customary units and record measurement equivalents.

> **Ounce (oz)** The weight of a slice of bread is about 1 ounce.
>
> **Pound (lb)** The weight of a loaf of bread is about 1 pound. There are 16 ounces in a pound.

1. What objects would be best weighed in ounces? What objects would be best weighed in pounds? Write two examples of each.

ounces: _____ _____

pounds: _____ _____

> **Fluid Ounce (fl oz)** One fluid ounce of liquid is about the amount that fits in a small medicine cup.
>
> **Cup (c)** One cup of liquid is about the amount that fits in a small glass. There are 8 fluid ounces in a cup.

2. When would liquids be best measured in fluid ounces? When would they be best measured in cups? Write two examples of each.

fluid ounces: _____ _____

cups: _____ _____

> **Inch (in)** The length of a small paperclip is about 1 inch.
>
> **Foot (ft)** The length of a large foot is about 12 inches. There are 12 inches in a foot.

3. What objects would be best measured in inches? What objects would be best measured in feet? Write two examples of each.

inches: _____ _____

feet: _____ _____

 Investigate: Look at the patterns below. Complete each table.

Weight

pound	ounces
1	16
2	32
3	
4	
5	80

Liquid Measure

cup	fluid ounces
1	8
2	
3	
	32
5	

Length

foot	inches
1	12
	24
3	
	48
5	

✏️ **Write About It:** On the back of the page, explain how to find the number of ounces in 10 pounds.

Investigate Math: Grade 4 © Cindi Mitchell, Scholastic Inc.

Compare relative sizes of metric units and record measurement equivalents.

Gram (g) The mass of a paper clip or a thumbtack is about 1 gram.

Kilogram (kg) The mass of a pineapple is about 1 kilogram. One kilogram equals 1,000 grams.

1. What objects would be best weighed in grams? What objects would be best weighed in kilograms? Write two examples of each.

grams: _____   _____

kilograms: _____   _____

Milliliter (ml) An eyedropper holds about a milliliter of liquid.

Liter (l) Water bottles hold about 1 liter of liquid. One liter equals 1,000 milliliters.

2. When would liquid volume be best measured in milliliters? When would it be best measured in liters? Write two examples of each.

milliliters: _____   _____

liters: _____   _____

Meter (m) The width of a door is about 1 meter.

Kilometer (km) The combined length of about 9 football fields is 1 kilometer. One kilometer equals 1,000 meters.

3. What lengths would be best measured in meters? What lengths would be best measured in kilometers? Write two examples of each.

meters: _____   _____

kilometers: _____   _____

Investigate: Look at the patterns below. Complete each table.

Mass		Liquid Volume		Length	
kilogram	grams	liter	milliliters	kilometer	meters
1	1,000	1	1,000	1	1,000
2		2			2,000
3	3,000	3		3	
4			4,000		4,000
5		5			5,000

 Write About It: On the back of the page, write a word problem that requires changing meters to kilometers. Be sure to include the solution.

#38 Name: _____

Use the four operations to solve word problems involving measurement.

Rosie has 2 pounds of fruit (see below) to divide between four baskets.

• 1 pound strawberries   • 8 ounces raspberries

• $\frac{1}{4}$ pound blueberries   • 4 ounces plums

How many ounces of each type of fruit should she put in each basket so that each basket weighs the same amount? Show two possible solutions.

Solution #1

Basket 1	Basket 2	Basket 3	Basket 4

Solution #2

Basket 1	Basket 2	Basket 3	Basket 4

 Investigate: Is it possible to evenly divide the fruit so that each basket is identical? Explain on the back of this page.

 Write About It: On the back of the page, write about the strategies you used to solve the problem.

#39 Name: _____

Use the four operations to solve word problems involving measurement.

Antonio wants to buy 7 feet of cord. The hardware store sells cord in 1-foot, 24-inch, 48-inch, or 5-foot packages.

1. How many of each package should he buy? Show three possible solutions.

Solution 1	Solution 2	Solution 3

2. Which solution results in buying the least number of packages? The greatest number?

_____

_____

3. Look at the pattern. Complete the table. Then, write a word problem that requires changing pounds to ounces.

pound	ounces
1	16
2	
	48
4	
5	

 Investigate: Write a question that can be answered by the information in the table above.

 Write About It: Give a step-by-step explanation of how you solved the problem at the top of the page.

Investigate Math: Grade 4 © Cindi Mitchell, Scholastic Inc.

#40 Name: _____

Solve real-world problems by applying area and perimeter formulas.

 You will need: colored pencils

Alex and Anthony design and make colorful tile hot plates. They use 36 two-inch square tiles of various colors for each plate.

1. Use the grids below to design two tile plates with different dimensions that each have 36 tiles. Use colored pencils to color the tiles and to create a design.

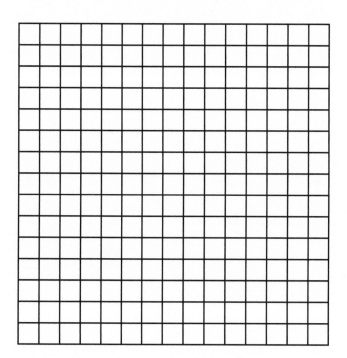 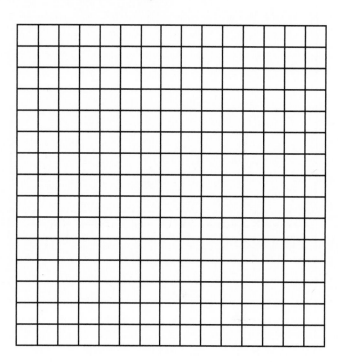

2. What are the dimensions of each plate?

_____

3. Alex and Anthony glue a thin strip of wood around each tile plate. How much wood will they need for each plate you designed? Explain.

_____

_____

 Investigate: If you know the area of a rectangular room and its length, can you figure out the width? Explain. Give an example to show your thinking.

Write About It: On the back of the page, define the term *perimeter* in your own words. What is one formula you can use to find the perimeter of a shape?

#41 Name: _____

Solve real-world problems by applying area and perimeter formulas.

Phyllis is getting a pygmy goat. She is drawing plans for a rectangular goat pen that has a perimeter of 720 feet.

1. Draw a diagram that shows the length and width of the rectangular goat pen. Show two possible solutions.

Solution 1

Solution 2

2. What is the area of each goat pen? What formula did you use to find the area?

_____

_____

🔍 **Investigate:** Is it possible for Phyllis to create a goat pen with four sides that are equal in length? Explain.

✏️ **Write About It:** On the back of the page, define the term *area* in your own words. Give an example.

Make a line plot to display a data set of measurements.

Look around the classroom. Find seven items that are less than 4 inches long.

1. List each object. Measure each length to the nearest $\frac{1}{4}$ inch and record.

Name of Object	Length

2. Order the data from least to greatest.

_____

3. Make a line plot using the measurement data you gathered.

Title _____

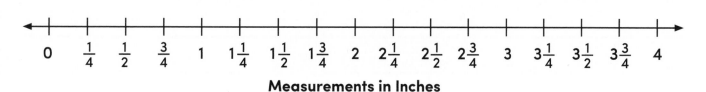

Measurements in Inches

 Investigate: Write three questions that can be answered with the information shown on the line plot.

 Write About It: On the back of the page, explain the purpose of a line plot.

Make a line plot to display a data set of measurements.

Create a line plot with measurement data you collect from your classmates.

• Choose a topic you want to investigate: shoe length, handspan, length of pinky finger, or wrist size.

• Measure and record data to the nearest $\frac{1}{8}$ inch.

Topic _____

Name of Person	Length	Name of Person	Length
1.		8.	
2.		9.	
3.		10.	
4.		11.	
5.		12.	
6.		13.	
7.		14.	

Make a line plot below to display the data.

 Investigate: On the back of the page, write three questions that can be answered with information from the line plot.

 Write About It: On the back of the page, describe when you would use a line plot in a real-life situation.

Investigate Math: Grade 4 © Cindi Mitchell, Scholastic Inc.

#44 Name: _____

Find out how degrees are related to fractional parts of a circle.

Look at the 360° circle. Use the information to answer the questions below.

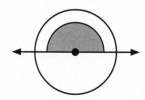

1. Look at the picture below to answer the following questions.

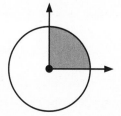

• What is the measure of the angle in degrees?   _____

• What fraction of the circle does the angle represent?   _____

• Write the measure of the angle as a fraction in which the numerator is the angle measurement and the denominator is 360.   _____

2. Look at the picture below to answer the following questions.

• What is the measure of the angle in degrees?   _____

• What fraction of the circle does the angle represent?   _____

• Write the measure of the angle as a fraction in which the numerator is the angle measurement and the denominator is 360.   _____

🔍 **Investigate:** Pierre draws an angle that is 225°. Eva says it measures $\frac{225}{360}$. Tom says it represents $\frac{5}{8}$ of the circle. Who is right? Explain.

✏️ **Write About It:** On the back of the page, write about an important idea you learned in the lesson. Explain why it is important.

#45 Name: _____

Measure angles in whole-number degrees using a protractor.

✓ **You will need** (for each player): blank sheet of paper • protractor • straightedge

Players: 2

Before You Play

Define each type of angle and draw an example.

acute angle	obtuse angle	right angle
_____	_____	_____

Play "Guess My Angle"

1. Each player uses a protractor and straightedge to draw an angle on a sheet of paper in secret. Each player labels his or her angle, writes its angle measure, and turns it facedown on the desk.

2. Players take turns asking yes or no questions to guess the measurement of the other player's mystery angle. Players should use terms like *acute* and *obtuse* to help narrow down the possible measurements.

3. The first person to guess the other player's mystery angle wins.

4. Grab another partner and play again.

 Investigate: Look around the classroom. Find familiar objects with various types of angles. Make a sketch of two of the items and share with a classmate.

 Write About It: On the back of the page, describe how to find an angle measure using a protractor.

#46 Name: _____

Measure angles in whole-number degrees using a protractor.

 You will need (for each player): 10 index cards • protractor • ruler • pencil

Players: 2

Before You Play

Each player creates matching game pieces using ten index cards. Here's how:

Take two index cards. On one index card, write the measurement of an angle. On the other index card, use a ruler and protractor to draw a model of the angle. Continue until you have five index cards that each show the measurement of an angle and five index cards that show a matching model of an angle.

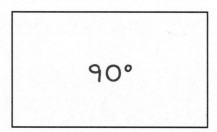   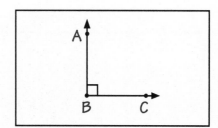

Play "Match-Up"

1. This game is similar to "Concentration." Combine cards with your partner and shuffle them. Then, place the cards in rows facedown on the desk.

2. Players take turns turning over two cards to find a match. If a possible match is found, the player uses a protractor to determine the exact measurement of the angle. If the angle measurement shown on one index card matches the protractor measurement of the model on the other index card, the player keeps the cards and takes another turn. If there is not a match, the player turns the cards back over. The other player takes a turn.

3. Play continues until all of the cards have been matched and picked up. The player with the most matches wins.

 Investigate: Find three different angles in the classroom. Guess and record the angle measure of each. Then, use a protractor to see if your guesses are correct and record.

Write About It: On the back of the page, explain how you would draw a 45° angle without using a protractor.

#47 Name: _____

Recognize angle measures as additive.

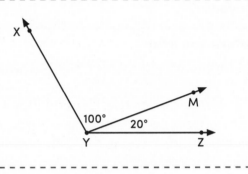

✓ **You will need:** protractor

Tom separated angle XYZ into two parts.
He used a protractor and measured each angle.
Then, he showed the angle measures
as a sum: 100° + 20° = 120°

1. Draw a model to show a different way to separate angle XYZ into two parts.

2. Show the angle measures as a sum: _____ + _____ = 120°

3. On the back of the page, draw a model to show how you could separate angle XYZ into three parts. Then, show the angle measures as a sum.

 Investigate: Freda is working on a design for a quilt. To start, she drew equal-sized angles in a circle and wrote the sum of the angle measures as an equation (see right). On the back of the page, show a different way that she could separate the circle into equal parts. Write the sum of the angle measures as an equation.

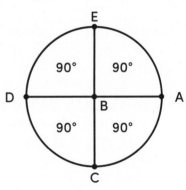

Write About It: On the back of the page, describe when you might use your knowledge of angles in real-life situations.

90° + 90° + 90° + 90° = 360°

Investigate Math: Grade 4 © Cindi Mitchell, Scholastic Inc.

#48 Name: _____

Solve addition and subtraction problems to find unknown angles.

 You will need: protractor

Angle ABC is 90°. Celeste separated the angle into two parts. She used a protractor and determined that angle TBC is 30°. To determine the measurement of the unknown angle, she wrote an equation and used a variable for the unknown angle measure.

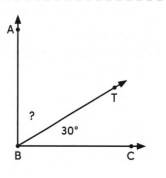

$x + 30° = 90°$ [Think 90° – 30° = 60°]

Angle ABT = 60°

1. Draw a model to show a different way to separate angle ABC into two parts. Label.

2. Use a protractor to find the measurement of one angle. _____

3. Write an equation to find the measurement of the other angle. Use a variable for the unknown angle measure. Then, solve the equation.

_____

 Investigate: On a separate sheet of paper, use a protractor to draw angle RST with a measure of 100°. Separate the angle into two parts and label. Identify the measurement of one angle. Write an equation to find the measurement of the other angle. Use a variable for the unknown angle measure. Swap with a classmate and identify each other's missing angle.

Write About It: On the back of the page, give some examples of professional workers who need to understand angles and geometry to do their everyday work.

#49 Name: _____

Draw points, lines, line segments, rays, and angles.

1. Look at the terms on the top row of the chart. Draw and label an example of each term. Then, list real-world examples that might represent each category. Finally, write a definition. The first one has been done for you.

Point	Line	Line Segment	Ray
● R • a period at the end of a sentence • the point on a pencil			
Definition A point is an exact location in space.	**Definition**	**Definition**	**Definition**

2. How are lines, line segments, and rays the same? How are they different?

_____

_____

_____

3. How are intersecting and parallel lines the same? How are they different?

_____

_____

Investigate: Draw a polygon that has at least one pair of parallel lines. Draw a polygon that has two pairs of parallel lines.

Write About It: Circle one of the figures you drew and labeled in the table above. Tell how you would say it and write about it.

Investigate Math: Grade 4 © Cindi Mitchell, Scholastic Inc.

#50 Name: _____

Draw points, lines, line segments, rays, and angles.

1. Look at the terms on the top row of the chart. Draw and label an example of each term. Then, list real-world examples that might represent each category. Finally, write a definition. The first one has been done for you.

Acute Angle	Obtuse Angle	Right Angle	Straight Angle
• $\frac{1}{8}$ piece of pie • hands on a clock that show 12:10 • scissors			
Definition An angle that measures less than 90°.	**Definition**	**Definition**	**Definition**

2. How are acute and obtuse angles the same? How are they different?

_____

_____

_____

Investigate: Draw a polygon with at least two obtuse angles. Draw another polygon with at least two acute angles.

Write About It: Circle one of the angles you drew and labeled in the table above. Tell three different ways you could describe it.

#51 Name: _____

Classify two-dimensional figures.

| trapezoid | parallelogram | rhombus | rectangle | square |

Choose two quadrilaterals from above to complete the table.

Write the name of the quadrilateral.		
Draw two pictures of the quadrilateral.		
What properties does the quadrilateral have? (*Think about its angles, length of sides, and number of parallel sides.*)		
Draw a picture of a non-example of the quadrilateral.		
Explain why the quadrilateral you drew is a non-example.		
Give real-life examples of this type of quadrilateral.		

 Investigate: Rachel says that all rectangles are quadrilaterals, and all quadrilaterals are rectangles. Is she correct? Explain.

 Write About It: On the back of the page, give an example of a quadrilateral that can be classified in more than one way. Explain why.

Investigate Math: Grade 4 © Cindi Mitchell, Scholastic Inc.

Classify two-dimensional figures.

Complete the table below.

	Acute Triangle	Obtuse Triangle	Right Triangle
Draw two examples of each type of triangle.			
What properties does the triangle have?			
Draw a picture of a non-example of the triangle.			
Explain why the triangle you drew is a non-example.			
Give real-life examples of this type of triangle.			

 Investigate: Answer each question below. Give examples, if possible.

- Can you draw a triangle that has more than one obtuse angle?

- Can you draw a triangle that has two right angles?

- Can you draw an angle without an obtuse angle?

 Write About It: On the back of the page, write three things you have learned about triangles in this lesson.

Identify lines of symmetry in figures and draw lines of symmetry.

✓ **You will need:** pattern blocks (at least one of each type of polygon)
• paper • pencil • scissors (optional)

> A line of symmetry is an imaginary line across a figure such that when you fold the figure in half, both halves match. Some figures have more than one line of symmetry.

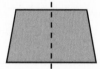

Choose two different pattern block shapes and trace around them. (You may want to trace the pattern blocks on a sheet of paper and cut them out. Then, you can fold the paper in various ways to see how many lines of symmetry you can find.) Draw all of the lines of symmetry in each shape.

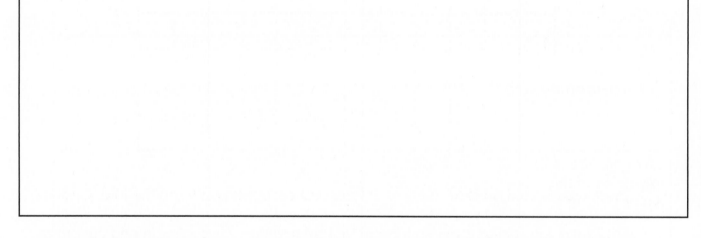

 Investigate: Look at the pattern block shapes. Which polygon has the most lines of symmetry? Draw a picture of the polygon and draw the lines of symmetry.

Which has the least? Draw a picture of the polygon and draw the lines of symmetry.

 Write About It: On the back of the page, give a few examples of symmetry that you notice in everyday life.

Investigate Math: Grade 4 © Cindi Mitchell, Scholastic Inc.

Identify lines of symmetry in figures and draw lines of symmetry.

 You will need: colored pencils

Artists often use symmetry to create designs. Color one half of the grid below to create a design of your choice. Then, give your design to a classmate to create a mirror image of it.

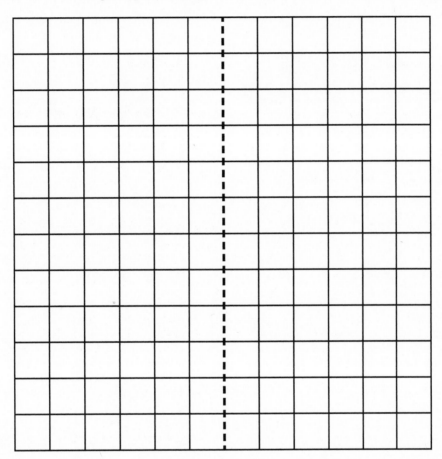

 Investigate: Fold a piece of paper in half and cut out a design on the fold. Open the paper. What did you notice about the cutout shape? What do you think would happen if you folded a piece of paper in half and then in half again and cut out a design? Try it.

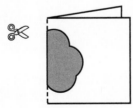

 Write About It: In your own words, define the term *symmetry*. Draw a figure that has no lines of symmetry.

Answer Key

#2 (page 8)
2. 6, 2, 3; 2 × 3 = 6
3. 15, 3, 5; 3 × 5 = 15
4. 12, 3, 4; 3 × 4 = 12

#3 (page 9)
1. ? × 4 = 20; Paul sold 5 cookies.
2. 1 × 4 = ?; popcorn costs 4 times as much as gummies.
3. 3 × ? = 12; Jarrod has 4 times more cows than Antonio.
4. 3 × ? = 18; Stewart gathered 6 eggs.

#4 (page 10)

Cows	Pigs	Chickens	Horses	Dogs	Cats
8	6	12	2	3	4

#11 (page 17)
3.
- 10 single blocks
- 10 strips of 10
- 10 100 blocks
- 10 1,000 blocks
- **Possible answer:** The models increase in size by 10.

Investigate: You would need 1,000 hundred blocks to model 100,000. Explanations will vary.

#16 (page 24)
Investigate: Rose's answer is incorrect. 3,992,199 rounded to the nearest ten thousand is 3,990,000.

#19 (page 27)
Investigate: If you use a standard number cube (1–6), the largest possible product is 3,996 (666 × 6) and the smallest possible product is 111 (111 × 1).

#20 (page 29)
Investigate:

	20	5
10	200	50
4	80	20

25 × 14 = 350

#25 (page 34)
1. T   **2.** T   **3.** T   **4.** F

#28 (page 37)
Investigate: Allen is incorrect. You cannot add together fractions that represent parts of shapes that are not identical.

#29 (page 38)
Investigate: $1\frac{4}{12}$ (or $1\frac{1}{3}$) carton

#30 (page 39)
Investigate: Milo walked less than 4 miles.
$4 \times \frac{2}{3} = 2\frac{2}{3}$ miles

#31 (page 40)
Investigate: $\frac{6}{10}$. Explanations will vary.

#32 (page 41)
1. $\frac{2}{10}$ or 0.2   **2.** $\frac{5}{10}$ or 0.5   **3.** $\frac{1}{10}$ or 0.1
Investigate: $\frac{2}{10}$, $\frac{6}{10}$, $\frac{8}{10}$, $\frac{9}{10}$; 0.1, 0.4, 0.6, 0.8

#33 (page 42)
1. $\frac{22}{100}$ or 0.22
2. $\frac{4}{100}$ or 0.04

#36 (page 45)
Investigate:

Weight		Liquid Measure		Length	
pound	ounces	cup	fluid ounces	foot	inches
1	16	1	8	1	12
2	32	2	16	2	24
3	48	3	24	3	36
4	64	4	32	4	48
5	80	5	40	5	60

#37 (page 46)
Investigate:

Mass		Liquid Volume		Length	
kilogram	grams	liter	milliliters	kilometer	meters
1	1,000	1	1,000	1	1,000
2	2,000	2	2,000	2	2,000
3	3,000	3	3,000	3	3,000
4	4,000	4	4,000	4	4,000
5	5,000	5	5,000	5	5,000

#38 (page 47)
Investigate: Yes, you can divide the fruit among the baskets evenly. Each basket will include 4 ounces of strawberries, 1 ounce of blueberries, 2 ounces of raspberries, and 1 ounce of plums.

#39 (page 48)
3.

pound	ounces
1	16
2	32
3	48
4	64
5	80

#40 (page 49)
Investigate: Yes, you can find the width of a rectangular room if you know its area and length. Area = length × width.

#41 (page 50)
Investigate: Yes, Phyllis's goat pen can have four sides of equal length. Each side would be 180 inches long.

#44 (page 53)
1. 180°, $\frac{1}{2}$, $\frac{180}{360}$ **2.** 90°, $\frac{1}{4}$, $\frac{90}{360}$
Investigate: Pierre and Eva are both right.
$\frac{225}{360}$ is $\frac{5}{8}$ of a circle.

#52 (page 61)
Investigate: No; no; yes. Examples will vary.

Investigate Math: Grade 4 © Cindi Mitchell, Scholastic Inc.